the COLLEC

To
Shapes

Judy Older and Louella Odié

SAGE
PRESS

Published in 2004

Text and Illustrations © Judy Older and Louella Odié
Design © Sage Press 2004

Set in Palatine italic 10 on 12 point leading.
Display in Palatino Light Italic 48 point.

Graphic Design
Chris Monk of Yellowduck Design Ltd

Text
Judy Older

Illustrations
Louella Odié

Series Editor and Publisher
Mrs Bobby Meyer

Printed in England

ISBN: 0-9542297-7-0

SAGE PRESS
PO Box Nº 1, Rye, East Sussex TN36 6HN.
e.mail: sagepress.bm@btinternet.com   www.sagepress.co.uk

In the beginning...

We have never been deterred by reality, it is more important to start with a vision than a plan

Topiary is a spiritually uplifting pastime, creative or wonderfully, cathartically destructive, depending on your mood and the sharpness of your shears. By introducing an element of fun and humour to your garden you transmit your personality to your borders.

Just as a well-fitting bra will improve an outfit, so topiary can be used as the foundation of a successful planting scheme. Trimming plants, shrubs and trees so that they do not encroach beyond their allotted space will result in structure throughout the seasons. Obviously evergreen shrubs are especially effective in the winter dusted with snow.

The clipped shapes become focal points either in pots or in the ground, enhancing the overall effect of your grand plan, with their bosomy contours or razor-edged precision, depending on your own personality.

Weaponry

Standard garden shears are fine for clipping hedges but topiary requires shears with fine blades. Lightweight garden shears made of aluminium with more pointed blades are widely available from large D.I.Y. stores and will give a more professional finish to your work.

True obsessives will cultivate the habit of pinching out growing shoots as they pass by

Sheep shears although generally recommended for topiary are best used for trimming sheep, or smaller leafed, established topiary to give a smooth finish.

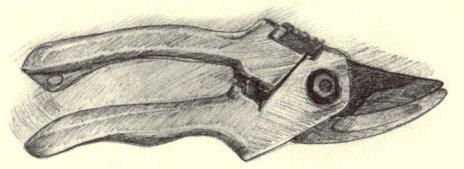

Larger leaved plants such as laurel and bay are best clipped using sharp secateurs. It is important to cut the stem, not the leaves, and angle your clipping action so that a softer, more pleasing finish is achieved. Avoid cutting larger leaves in half and producing a maimed look.

Be prepared to let common sense be overridden by your enthusiasm, the results of your spontaneous creativity may surprise you

Achievable shapes for beginners

A round shape is the easiest to begin with, as you can hack away on a multi-branched, small leaved plant such as box, yew, lonicera nitida or euonymus and quite successfully arrive at a design near enough the one you first thought of, e.g. an egg.

Place a cloth around the base of the plant to catch the clippings. Make the first cut along the top of the branch having decided on the finished height that you are aiming for. Clip around the sides a little at a time with the shears pointing away from you. Turn the pot, or keep moving around the plant to ensure a balanced shape. Lastly trim under the lower edge to round off. Create a cube by the same method but clip the sides and the top flat.

Knowing when to stop clipping is the key to success

A layer of fine gravel to a depth of $\frac{1}{2}$" (1cm) finishes off and 'presents' the plant whilst indicating that however it looks, it was exactly what you intended

Illusions of Grandeur

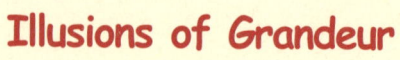

Choose a tall plant that has a strong, vertical, central stem and bushy side shoots. This will help you achieve a satisfyingly dense finish. A tip for the less confident amongst you is to give yourself a lead start and buy a tall, thick, dense cone to start off with.

No-one will know about this perfectly acceptable ruse and you then can swiftly customise it and claim all the credit when the compliments flow.

Shapes for the confident

Ideally shrubs no shorter than 39" (1m) will be used. Small-leaved box, yew, leylandii, goldcrest and pittisporum, as well as ligustrum and viburnum tinus all make suitable subjects.

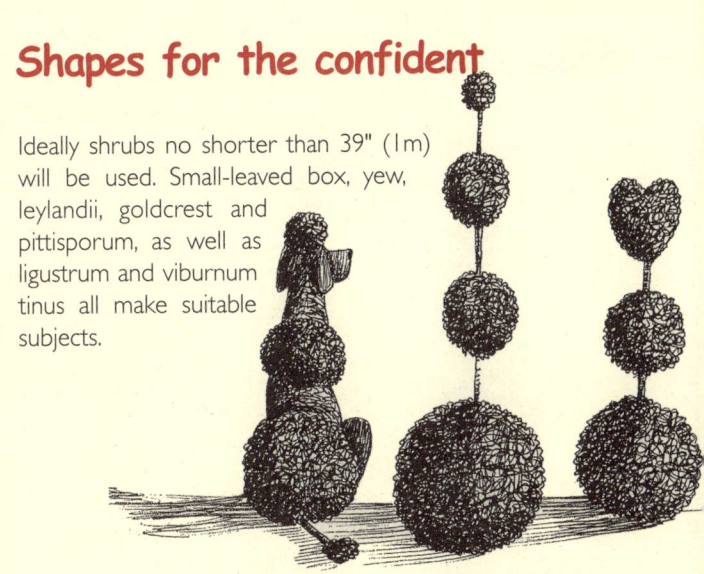

For a poodle trim decide on how many balls or layers you want. As a rule you can cut three balls or layers per 3' approx (1m) of shrub. Clip the lowest/largest ball or layer to the required size and shape. Then above the first ball trim. Then trim the side shoots back to the main stem leaving at least a 3" (7.5cm) gap between the layers. Clip thus until you reach the top. Next year cup as before and repeat as necessary.

Do step back from the piece regularly to ensure the shape is balanced and that the spaces in between are equidistant.

Shapes to impress

Spirals are daunting to begin with, but it is easier if you can start with a ready-shaped box cone (or something similar).

Attach a length of contrasting string or ribbon to one side of the pot or tie string to a skewer and insert into the ground on one side of the chosen shrub.

The plant should ideally be no less than 39" (1m) in height (although see tiny topiary page 25). Wind the string around the plant's outline, not tight enough to cut into the shape but again not so loosely that the ribbon will slip (see opposite).

The slope of the ribbon should spiral at an angle of about 45° and complete a circuit every 1' (30 cm).

The much-maligned Leylandii, especially chamecyparis 'Golden King', looks terrific spiralled in this way.

Cut in towards the main stem, starting from the bottom, right or left, and working along the string line. The deeper you cut, the more defined the shape will be. If the plant is in a pot, turn it around as you work to keep the shape balanced.

Finally, trim with the tips of the shears to even out curves.

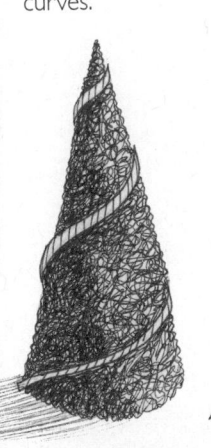 

Whether to cut all the way in and expose the central stem or not is a question of personal preference. We feel that an exposed stem is more suitable for Italianate or formal settings and is the 'super-model' of topiary, compared to the softer cottage garden spiral with its comfortable folds.

Standards: Tomorrow is another Bay

There is an enormous choice of plants for standardising. Bay is often used but holly, leylandii, myrtle, laurel and tinus all make good specimens.

Other plants such as wisteria and honeysuckle may be trained into standards by tying the main stem to a stout cane and pinching out the top at the desired height. Then remove the unwanted side shoots from the stem, leaving a good bushy top. Tight clip only after flowering. Non-flowering shrubs may be closely trimmed into balls, cubes or lollipops.

Select a plant with a suitable central stem and trim off the lower shoots at the base of the shape up to the desired height. Clip the remaining shoots into a ball, cube or any 'lollipop shape'.

Trimming tips

Trimming should ideally be done between May and October, depending on climatic conditions; it is important not to clip during frosty weather, nor on a scorching day. In reality, however, the topiary fanatic surrenders to the overwhelming urge to tweak even the perfectly manicured subject obsessively! Some shrubs require more attention than others to maintain a good shape. Lonicera nitida, for instance, requires almost a weekly haircut to keep that velvet finish.

Here are some approximate guidelines:
Box – mid-June and September
Leylandii – June and September
Yew – August
Lavender – Once in the spring and again after flowering, but not into the old wood – although personal experience shows it not to affect the plant. It should be remembered that lavender is in fact a very short-lived plant anyway: the average life is around five years.

Wisteria– Back to every third bud in February. Long, whippy shoots need shortening or removing in August. Individual specimens may require specific maintenance: holly produces fewer berries if clipped regularly. Do not clip laurels tinus after July if you require flowers and berries.

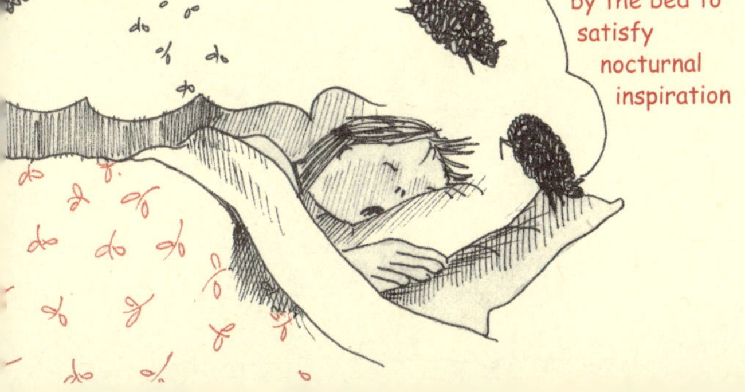

We recommend that wellies, torch and clippers should be conveniently left by the bed to satisfy nocturnal inspiration

Corsetry and Bondage

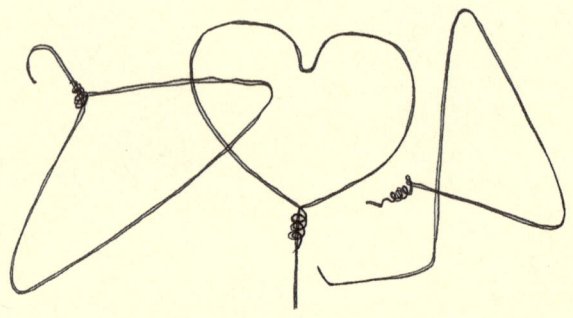

Although there are many types of commercial frames available, a simple outline can be made from a wire coat hanger or a length of wire, which may be easier to use than the cage type of frame.

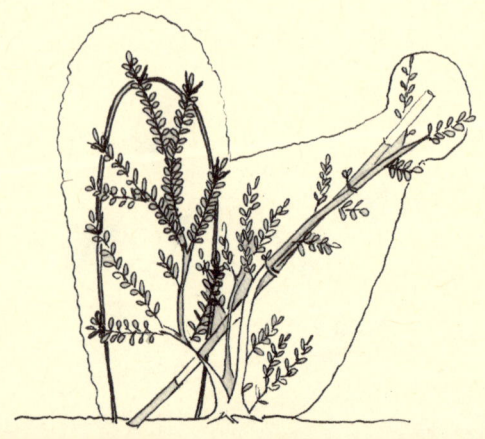

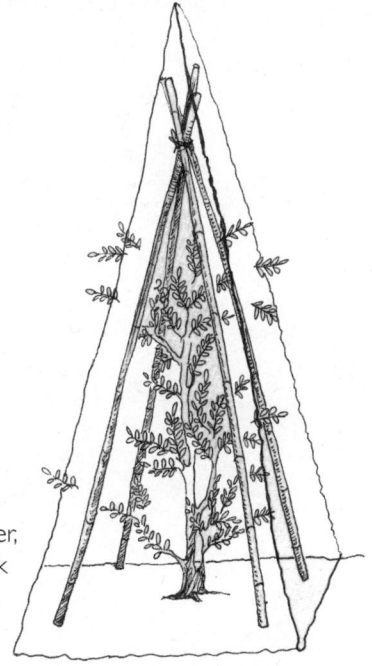

If using a coat hanger, straighten the hook and reduce its length by half, pull the hanger into the desired shape, (ball, triangle, heart, bird or rabbit) and insert into the flower pot as close to the stem as possible. Then tie the outline shape to the plant at intervals.

Trim back any shoots that grow above the wire and round down any stems either side of the outline. Canes or sticks stuck into the ground may be used to pull branches down to the required direction or angle, in particular for peacocks and pheasants. Over time their angles become permanent as will your back.

Hedera Helix
Ivy to you and me

Long trails of ivy produce a swifter result than box, but never really attain the same smooth contours. All varieties, small or large leaved, may be used. Small leaves of course will make a smoother outline. A frame or wire netting will be needed for the support.

Tie the ivy trails to the frame at intervals, and then remove any unwanted shoots as they grow to keep the shape neat.

If you aim to produce an instant ivy spiral you will require a plant with trails three times the height of the frame. Start by winding the ivy round the frame, tying it in at regular intervals. Keep the ivy on the outside of the frame and do not entwine the ivy with the wire.

Trellis or chains are also suitable for supporting ivy, but once again tie the ivy to the chain so that it can be removed and the design changed. Trim constantly to maintain the shape.

Greater things or even bigger Mistakes

Established borders may contain larger shrubs which have the potential to be enhanced by manicuring. Evergreen shrubs make the best subjects, for example: laurel, holly, viburnam tinus, euonymous and skimmia.

Examine the shrubs in your garden to determine their individual strengths. Plants with strong vertical stems could be encouraged to form cones, obelisks and pillars, whereas bushier plants will make successful spherical shapes.

Cutting back in the winter months to a more formal framework will give you a base to work from. Regular trimming over time will then lead to greater density and visual impact in the border or along the pathway. Remember, though, this may reveal focal points previously hidden, sometimes deliberately!

Shopping for Shape, using your Imagination

The secret of success with individual topiary shapes lies in carefully examining and observing the structure of a plant and visualising its potential. With practice you will be unable to pass any shrubs by without fantasising about topiary possibilities – friends' gardens will be full of temptations. There's no need to resist a whole new canvas, but ask for permission first!

Remember that formal classic geometric designs are best when trained to a shape over a period of time, rather than being cut out from bigger shrubs. If done too quickly they will lack the density and strength of a couple of years growth.

For animals and birds, try looking at other plants than box and yew. We suggest a visit to a specialist hedging nursery. Seek out the more straggly specimens and you will immediately see possibilities. In the same vein, smaller leaved shrubs such as myrtle, and lonicera, also known as 'poor man's box', are worth considering with the same aim in mind

Tiny Topiary

For the small-minded – window boxes and balconies:

A steady hand is required when producing tiny topiary, as there is less room for error. Shapes may be as simple or as intricate as you wish but the use of very small-leaved evergreen plants is essential. Euonymous, lonicera nitida and box are ideal.

Packs of small box plants, which are commercially produced, 5-6" (15cm) in height or alternatively homegrown cuttings, supported by a thin cane may be cut into balls, cones, or cubes and are ideal for window boxes and pots for year-round interest. They can achieve the same look of formality and rhythm as larger specimens in a border.

Pairs of matching spirals or standards are more elegant than just one.

For optimum health container topiary will need more care and attention and regular feeding than those in open ground. Do remember to put gravel around the base surfaces for a smarter effect and to reduce water loss. Make sure vunerable topiary is secure in a strong wind.

Potty training

The advantage of topiary created from large potted shrubs is that they may be sited strategically according to the seasons. In addition, flowering topiary made from jasmine spirals would not only provide definition to a door or gateway, but also have the added bonus of perfuming the air.

For greater impact, group three different-sized, similar-shaped pieces in matching containers. Family groups look far friendlier and overall produce a more attractive impact than single plants dotted around the garden.

Equally, pairs of matching spirals or standards are far more elegant than just one on its own.

Position is everything

If space is restricted by your garden size, ie. in a courtyard or a balcony garden, and the topiary has to stand against a wall or trellis, consider an evergreen or small-flowered shrub or fruit tree for greater seasonal interest. Escalonia, cotoneaster or hydrangea paniculata have extended interest with their flowers and berries. Apple trees may be used in espalier form against a wall, restricting the growth to the space available. Secure firmly with vine eyes hammered into the wall.

Cotoneaster may be trained into an arch over a door or around a window frame and clipped regularly.

The length of time it takes to surround a doorway or window of course depends upon the size of the plant you start with. Large plants are available which could encourage you to achieve a near instant effect, althouth it would obviously take longer for the plant to fill out.

Camouflaging Errors with confidence ... Or turning a Topiary Disaster into a Triumph

An important early lesson

1.   Buy more plants than you need, in case you maim the piece you are working on. You can easily turned a failed spiral into a three balled poodle tail but not the other way round.

2.   If mistakes are made by over-enthusiastic clipping, remember that like hair it will usually grow back and cover your errors. Be positive about this for you may even create a better shape than originally planned.

3.   Imperfections in a spiral or poodle tail shape may be rectified by careful positioning in the garden i.e. in the darkest corner or where they will be seen from one side only.

If challenged, be confident with your explanations and remember each piece of topiary is unique and has its own character created by you. Do not be too ambitious, start small and work up, although perhaps a piece of topiary involving a ladder is obviously too big for most of us and should be avoided.

Small is beautiful and less is more.

Don't be afraid to express the inner Yew

Use your business as a showcase for your artistry

Bring out the child in you

The Collector's Series of Trees

Are you collecting…?

"… and a very charming book it is…"

Roy Lancaster,
on MONKEY PUZZLE